GRAPHIC LIBRARY™

GRAPHIC SCIENCE

THE DYNAMIC WORLD OF CHEMICAL REACTIONS

WITH **MAX AXIOM** SUPER SCIENTIST ®

Agnieszka Biskup

illustrated by Cynthia Martin

and Barbara Schulz

Raintree

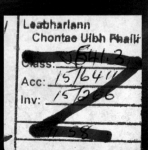

www.raintreepublishers.co.uk
Visit our website to find out
more information about
Raintree books.

To order:
☎ Phone 0845 6044371
🖹 Fax +44 (0) 1865 312263
✉ Email myorders@raintreepublishers.co.uk

Customers from outside the UK please telephone +44 1865 312262

Raintree is an imprint of Capstone Global Library Limited, a company
incorporated in England and Wales having its registered office at 7 Pilgrim Street,
London, EC4V 6LB – Registered company number: 6695582

Designers: Alison Thiele and Victoria Allen
Colourist: Matt Webb
Cover artists: Tod Smith and Krista Ward
Media researcher: Wanda Winch
Editors: Christopher Harbo and Diyan Leake
Originated by Capstone Global Library Limited
Printed and bound in China by South China Printing Company Limited

ISBN 978 1 406 22581 5 (hardback)   ISBN 978 1 406 22585 3 (paperback)
14 13 12 11 10   15 14 13 12 11
10 9 8 7 6 5 4 3 2 1   10 9 8 7 6 5 4 3 2 1

British Library Cataloguing in Publication Data
Biskup, Agnieszka. The dynamic world of chemical reactions. -- (Graphic science)
541.3'9-dc22
A full catalogue record for this book is available from the British Library.

CONTENTS

SECTION 1

REACTIONS AROUND US --------- 4

SECTION 2

MATTER, ATOMS, AND MOLECULES --- 8

SECTION 3

CHANGING MATTER --------------- 14

SECTION 4

DYNAMIC REACTIONS ----------- 22

More about chemical reactions and Max Axiom.............28–29
Glossary... 30
Find out more... 31
Index 32

But fire isn't the only chemical reaction you can see.

From exploding fireworks to flashing fireflies, we're surrounded by chemical changes all the time.

To understand chemical reactions, you have to understand matter.

Matter makes up everything in the Universe.

Galaxies, stars, and planets are all made of matter.

Everything alive is made of matter, including plants, animals, you, and me.

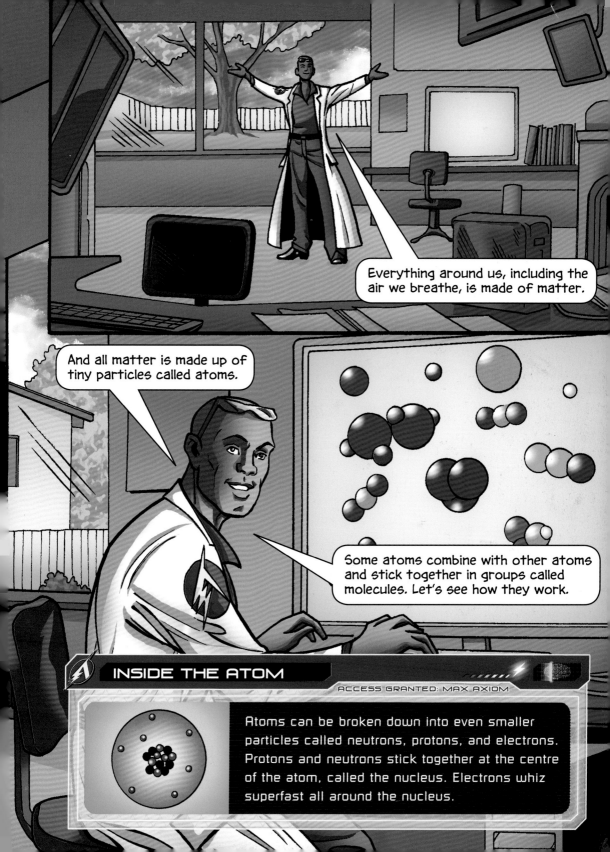

Imagine taking a drop of water and splitting it in two.

Now split it again ...

... and again and again.

Eventually you'd split the drop down to a single molecule of water.

H

H

O

And if you looked closely, you'd see its basic structure. A water molecule is made up of one oxygen atom and two hydrogen atoms.

TINY, TINY ATOMS

It can be mind-boggling to think about the very small size of atoms. There can be a few sextillion (a 1 followed by 21 zeros) atoms in a drop of water. Can you imagine 1,000,000,000,000,000,000,000 of anything?

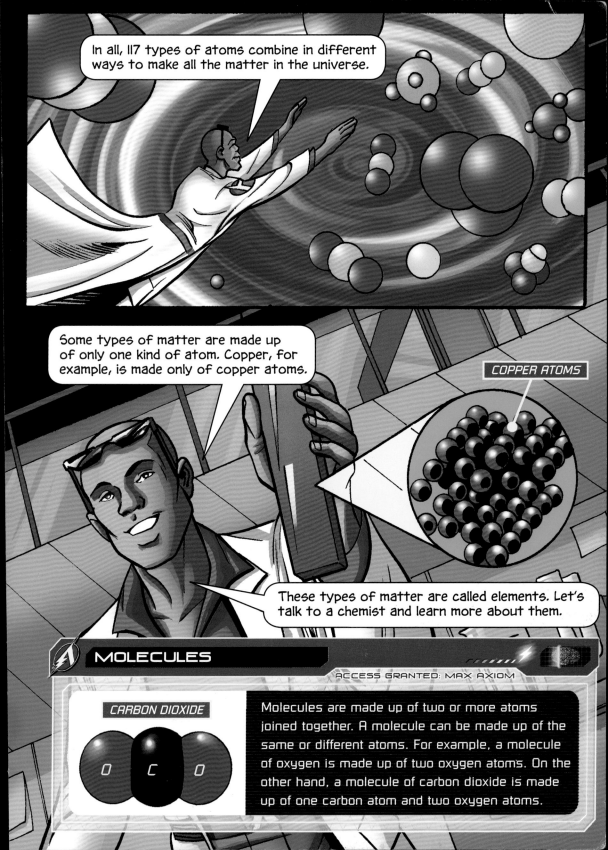

In all, 117 types of atoms combine in different ways to make all the matter in the universe.

Some types of matter are made up of only one kind of atom. Copper, for example, is made only of copper atoms.

COPPER ATOMS

These types of matter are called elements. Let's talk to a chemist and learn more about them.

MOLECULES

ACCESS GRANTED: MAX AXIOM

CARBON DIOXIDE

O C O

Molecules are made up of two or more atoms joined together. A molecule can be made up of the same or different atoms. For example, a molecule of oxygen is made up of two oxygen atoms. On the other hand, a molecule of carbon dioxide is made up of one carbon atom and two oxygen atoms.

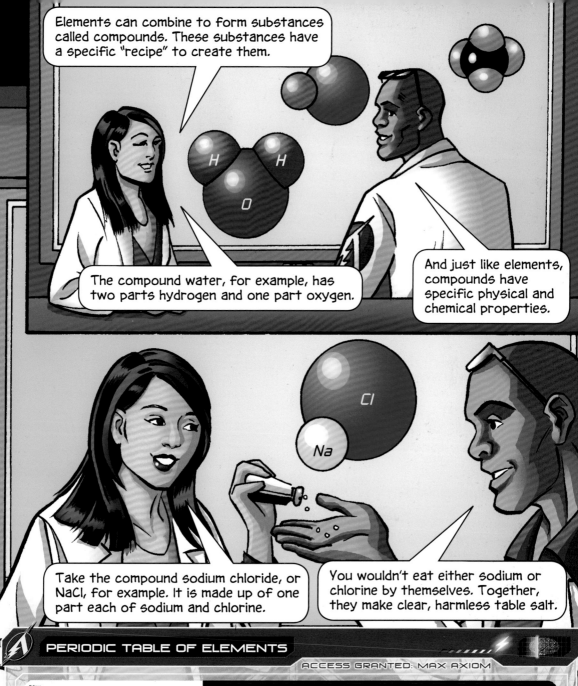
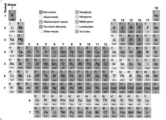

Matter can change in two ways.

It can have a physical change or a chemical change.

Physical changes only change the physical properties of a substance. Its chemical make-up stays the same.

I can crumple a piece of paper. But it's still paper.

I can hammer gold into a different shape, but it remains gold with the same chemical properties it had before.

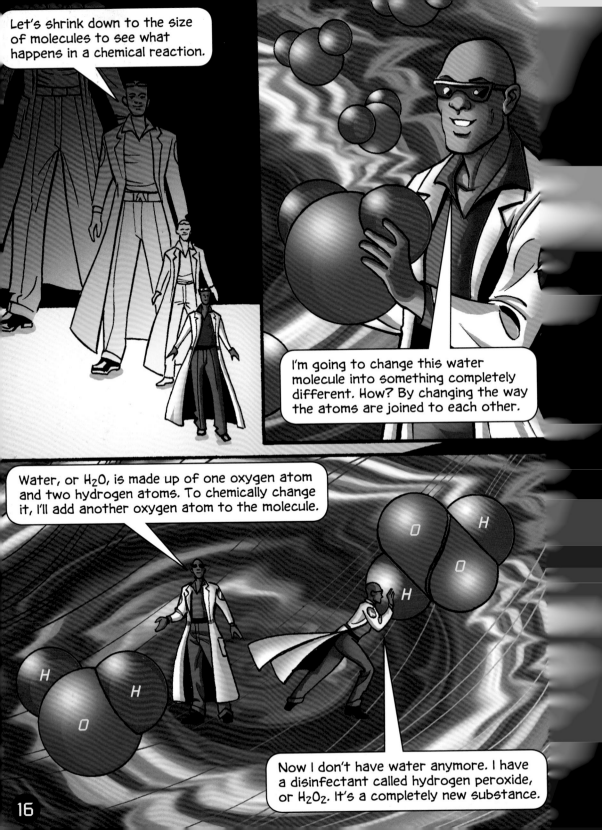

Let's shrink down to the size of molecules to see what happens in a chemical reaction.

I'm going to change this water molecule into something completely different. How? By changing the way the atoms are joined to each other.

Water, or H_2O, is made up of one oxygen atom and two hydrogen atoms. To chemically change it, I'll add another oxygen atom to the molecule.

Now I don't have water anymore. I have a disinfectant called hydrogen peroxide, or H_2O_2. It's a completely new substance.

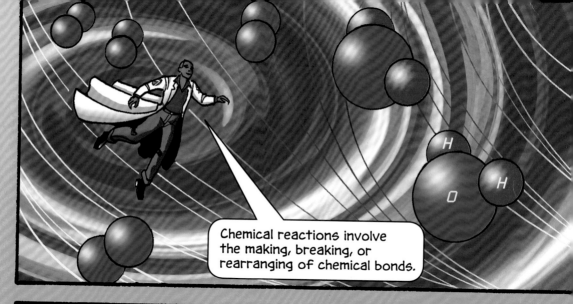

Chemical reactions involve the making, breaking, or rearranging of chemical bonds.

Chemical bonds hold the atoms in a molecule together. These bonds are sometimes formed by the atoms' outermost electrons.

ELECTRONS

NUCLEUS

WATER MOLECULE

In a water molecule, the hydrogen atoms share their electrons with the oxygen atom.

REACTANTS AND PRODUCTS

In a chemical reaction, the substances that undergo a chemical change are called the reactants. The substances that result from the change are called the products.

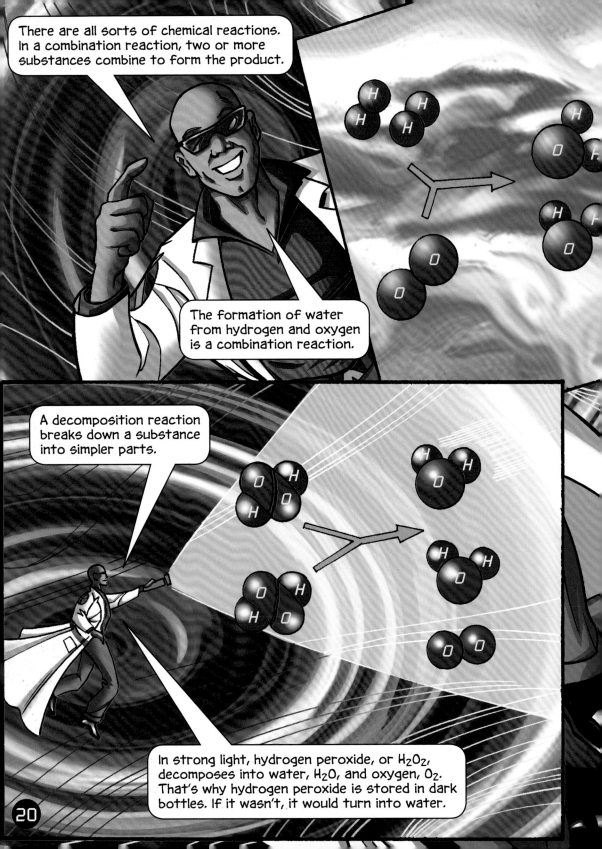

There are all sorts of chemical reactions. In a combination reaction, two or more substances combine to form the product.

The formation of water from hydrogen and oxygen is a combination reaction.

A decomposition reaction breaks down a substance into simpler parts.

In strong light, hydrogen peroxide, or H_2O_2, decomposes into water, H_2O, and oxygen, O_2. That's why hydrogen peroxide is stored in dark bottles. If it wasn't, it would turn into water.

Depending on whether chemical bonds are broken or formed, a reaction can give off heat or take in heat.

Chemical reactions that take in energy are called endothermic reactions.

Photosynthesis is an endothermic reaction. During photosynthesis, plants take in energy from the Sun and use it to make food.

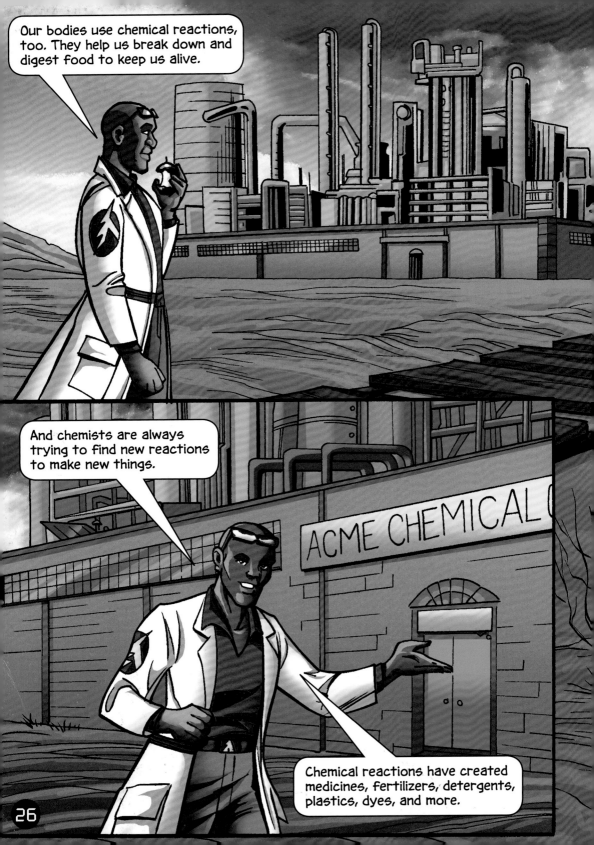

CHEMICAL REACTIONS

Elements are the simplest forms of matter. There are 117 known elements in the universe. About 90 of these elements are found naturally on Earth or in the atmosphere. The others have been created in laboratories. Scientists are still working on discovering new elements.

A molecular formula tells you the total number and kinds of atoms in a molecule. Water's molecular formula is H_2O. That means to make a molecule of water you need two atoms of hydrogen (H) and one atom of oxygen (O). Carbon dioxide's formula is CO_2. That means you'd need one atom of carbon (C) and two of oxygen (O) to make a carbon dioxide molecule.

Fireflies glow because of a special reaction involving oxygen atoms and two other chemicals. The chemical reaction takes place in the firefly's abdomen. The light produced shines right through its body.

Heating chemical compounds produces the beautiful colours you see in fireworks. When heated, the compounds give off colours. To get blue, fireworks experts add copper compounds. To get orange, they add calcium.

Many copper roofs are green thanks to chemical reactions. They are originally the colour of 1p and 2p coins. But over the years, the copper has reacted with oxygen in the air, or oxidized, to form a green coating.

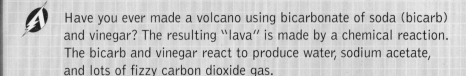

Have you ever made a volcano using bicarbonate of soda (bicarb) and vinegar? The resulting "lava" is made by a chemical reaction. The bicarb and vinegar react to produce water, sodium acetate, and lots of fizzy carbon dioxide gas.

Acid rain is caused by sulphur dioxide and nitrogen oxides that are released into the atmosphere by human pollution or natural events. These chemicals react with water, oxygen, and other compounds to form acid rain. Acid rain has harmful effects on the environment, wildlife, and humans.

MORE ABOUT

SUPER SCIENTIST

Real name: Maxwell Axiom
Height: 1.86 m (6 ft 1 in.)
Weight: 87 kg (13 st. 10 lb)
Eyes: Brown **Hair:** None

Super capabilities: Super intelligence; able to shrink to the size of an atom; sunglasses give x-ray vision; lab coat allows for travel through time and space.

Origin: Since birth, Max Axiom seemed destined for greatness. His mother, a marine biologist, taught her son about the mysteries of the sea. His father, a nuclear physicist and volunteer park warden, showed Max the wonders of Earth and sky.

One day while Max was hiking in the hills, a megacharged lightning bolt struck him with blinding fury. When he awoke, Max discovered a new-found energy and set out to learn as much about science as possible. He travelled the globe studying every aspect of the subject. Then he was ready to share his knowledge and new identity with the world. He had become Max Axiom, Super Scientist.

GLOSSARY

atom element in its smallest form

combination reaction chemical reaction where two substances combine to form a new product

combustion the process of catching fire and burning

compound something formed by combining two or more parts

decomposition reaction chemical reaction where a substance breaks down into simpler parts

electron tiny particle in an atom that travels around the nucleus

element basic substance in chemistry that cannot be broken down into simpler substances under ordinary lab conditions

endothermic reaction chemical reaction that takes in energy

exothermic reaction chemical reaction that gives off energy

fermentation chemical change that makes the sugar in a substance change into alcohol

matter anything that has weight and takes up space

molecule two or more atoms of the same or different elements that have bonded. A molecule is the smallest part of a substance that can not be divided without a chemical change.

FIND OUT

Books

Building Blocks of Matter series, Louise and Richard Spilsbury (Heinemann Library, 2008)

Changing Materials (Understanding Science), Penny Johnson (Schofield and Sims, 2007)

Changing States: Solids, Liquids, and Gases (Do It Yourself), Will Hurd (Heinemann Library, 2010)

Fireworks!: Changing Materials (Fusion: Physical Processes and Materials), Isabel Thomas (Raintree, 2007)

How to be a Scientist, Susan Glass (Heinemann Library, 2008)

Marie Curie and Radioactivity (Graphic Inventions and Discovery), Connie Miller (Raintree, 2010)

The Solid Truth about States of Matter (Graphic Science), Agnieszka Biskup (Raintree, 2010)

Websites

www.bbc.co.uk/schools/ks3bitesize/science
Click on "Chemical and material behaviour" for activities and to discover more about atoms.

www.tryscience.org/experiments/experiments_home.html
Click on the chemistry topic for experiments you can try at home.

acid rain, 29
atoms, 9, 10–11, 15, 16, 17, 18, 19, 28

burning, 4, 7, 17, 24, 25

carbon, 11, 13, 18, 28
carbon dioxide, 6, 11, 18, 27, 28, 29
chemical bonds, 19, 22
chlorine, 12, 13
combination reactions, 20
combustion. *See* burning
compounds, 13, 18, 28, 29
copper, 11, 28

decomposition reactions, 20
digestion, 6, 26

electrons, 9, 19
elements, 11, 12–13, 28
endothermic reactions, 22
energy, 22, 23, 24
exothermic reactions, 23, 24
explosions, 23

fermentation, 6
fire, 4–5, 6, 24–25
fireflies, 5, 28
fireworks, 5, 7, 28

gunpowder, 7

heat, 15, 22, 23, 24, 25, 28
hydrogen, 10, 13, 16, 19, 20, 28
hydrogen peroxide, 16, 20

matter, 8–9, 11, 14, 21, 28
molecules, 9, 10, 11, 15, 16, 19, 28

oxygen, 10, 11, 13, 16, 18, 19, 20, 24, 25, 28, 29

periodic table of elements, 13
photosynthesis, 22
physical changes, 14–15
products, 18, 19, 20, 21

reactants, 19, 21
rust, 25

sodium, 12, 13
sodium chloride, 13

table salt. *See* sodium chloride

water, 10, 13, 15, 16, 17, 19, 20, 25, 28, 29